REFUGEE SONG

# REFUGEE SONG

## LAWRENCE FEUCHTWANGER

*VANCOUVER, MAY 4, 2016*

*FOR CHRIS.*

*LAWRENCE*

George Payerle, Editor

*Signature*
**EDITIONS**

Cover design by Doowah Design.
Photo of Lawrence Feuchtwanger by Sarah Hollett.

This book was printed on Ancient Forest Friendly paper.
Printed and bound in Canada by Hignell Book Printing Inc.

We acknowledge the support of The Canada Council for the Arts and the Manitoba Arts Council for our publishing program.

**Library and Archives Canada Cataloguing in Publication**

Feuchtwanger, Lawrence, 1952-, author
    Refugee song / Lawrence Feuchtwanger.

Poems.
ISBN 978-1-927426-41-8 (pbk.)

    I. Title.

PS8611.E927R43 2014     C811'.6     C2014-900946-1

Signature Editions
P.O. Box 206, RPO Corydon, Winnipeg, Manitoba, R3M 3S7
www.signature-editions.com

*For Debbie*


*In memory of my parents*

# CONTENTS

UNTIL IT IS SUNG
    Incantation    13

THIS CLEFT PALATE
    Call    17
    Fugue    20

JUST PASSING THROUGH
    Da Capo    25
    Segue    27
    Caesura    28
    Segue (cont'd)    31

SUNT LACRIMAE RERUM
    Prayer    35
    Lament    38

THE EARTH OPENING
    Echo    43
    Paean    44

O, HOW THEY LOVED ME
    Blessing    49
    Ligature    50
    Lullaby    51
    Quaver (Penelope)    52
    Elegy    54
    Lullaby II    55

THE PLACES SHE DIDN'T TOUCH ME
    Bridge    59
    Siren Song    61

## THE GATES HAVE WINGS

Descant                    65
Psalm                      67
Kaddish                    69

## MY HEART, SURFACING TOO FAST

Harmony                    73
Anthem (O Canada)          76
Cry                        79
Cadence                    81


Key                        83
Acknowledgements           88
About the Author           89

*Oh what greater happiness*
      *Could you have than this:*
*After reaching land to lie down*
            *Under the eaves to sleep*
*And hear the steady small*
            *Rain in your thoughts*

— Sophocles

# UNTIL IT IS SUNG

# Incantation

*Song, when it comes,*
*comes crawling on childhood's knees,*
*torn and tender*

*comes blowing across the burning veld,*
*cradled in wind's cracked palm,*
*sheds its charred skin,*
*scattering cadence and scale.*

*Song, when it calls,*
*calls me back*
*with its half-truths and half-lies, its half-promises*
*to pick out the sliver from the sinew,*
*the slip from the tongue,*
*the needle from the junkie's arm.*

*Song moistens my parched lips,*
*fills in the blanks,*
*sucks the poison from my wounds,*
*kneels, and gives thanks.*

*Song stares through the empty window*
*out into the schoolyard,*
*runs its captive fingers across the names*
*scarred into the desktop*

*slips its restraints,*
*slips out through the back door,*
*spills into the riotous streets,*
*dances in the shanty shade*
*until it is beaten back.*

*Song sinks into waves' gentle lap,*
*into farewells and horizons,*
*into tidal longing.*

*Listen,*
*as it makes landfall,*
*washes up on shoreline's lips,*
*catches in ear's cuckold shell.*

*Listen for its torn turn of phrase,*
*to the sinned for and against.*
*Listen for the foetal curl,*
*to the plucked umbilic note.*

*Listen*
*for the small song*
*inside the song.*

*Listen*

*for, until it is sung,*
*until it is heard,*

# THIS CLEFT PALATE

## Call

I rise early, into a fine December drizzle.

Descend through the damp, down
to a place below the place where the river splits
in two,
towards its languid mouth, carelessly spilled secrets.

The almost emptied year lies mostly behind us,
the dark century beginning to close in on itself,
within sight of understanding.

My gaze, tilting westward, leans
into earth's curve, falls back...

This is both before
and after.

The world has grown smaller, and because small,
is held close,
and because close, is sometimes unseen.
The aging millennium has been blinded
by what it has been witness to.

But still, prisoners of conscience
grown grey with memory
have walked through walls, seen the rainbow fade.

*I* see now, that although history has unfolded
without me, the ever-receding past remains
ever-present,
graffiti ghosting through insoluble lines, redacted truths,
visible only to the naked.

So, when I say, *my* country,
I no longer know what I mean, or
even what I mean to say.

Do I mean the endless stretch and certainty
of a cloudless *lowveld* sky,
marching rows of *mielies* dropping their tassled heads
to pray for rain?

Or, do I mean this rip in the evergreen,
heaven's tears pouring through, day and night,
granting cedar its rough promise, salmon its blind leap?

Or, do I simply mean to ask you
to help me arrange these cut *proteas*
in this cut-glass vase, so that their dried hearts can drink?

A drying mouth goes in search of a river,
an empty socket in search of a skull,
a wound in search of a knife.

I go through too neat streets in search
of homeland security, the comfort
of familiar foes
amongst the city's uprooted faces.
Before time can move forward, I must return
to unbury the dead,
interrupt their half-life decay

before the score's erased,
must follow the phantom limb's fading song,
pluck each careful note
from each uncertain tongue.

And, because this body, creased as it is,
is the only surviving map,
I ask again that you unfold it with care.

Because this crumbling parchment
is all that I have left of the truth, I beg you,
come lie with me.

I have come as far as I possibly can.

If it is easy to recount how I find myself here
—a derailing, a failure of heart, sudden flight—
it is harder to count all that has been lost.

This sea-level depression lifts,
a dull light reflecting off water's weal
as it swells towards the ocean.

But because an ocean cannot wash the salt
from its own wounds,
I must again step into these waters,
cross this continental divide, this cleft palate
into fatherland
and motherland,
brotherland
and otherland

cross and uncross
before the fading light
covers us in darkness, again.

## Fugue

Return is exile,
to and from,
doing and undoing time,
crossing parallels.

*Who is that calling?*

Sit still,
be transported.
Weave, unravel, pour day back
into night.
Untell this story.

This shaky craft
lifts
on a rising tide of longing, towards a promise of land,
a scallop of earth,
somewhere

lists against the flawed logic of the senses,
tugs at gravity's embrace,
as the things that hold me here — wife, child —
lose depth.

The world unfurls.

The world up against itself,
sharp upthrust,
geological accident, ancient and imminent.
On the cusp of an invisible sea,
the city, still barely asleep.

The Fraser River, reaching for home,
looses herself.
Penelope, rooted to her wanton bed,
hand spread across her delta
to ward off the unwanted loneliness of loyalty.

Far below, plains bleed,
fractal islands weep.

A buried narrative,
indifference of ocean ripples on mountaintops
spilling white,
something to cry over.

*What has put me here?*

Midway between there and here;
death.

The end of something,
due date on a refugee nightmare,
return to red earth.

In this pressurized steel curve,
doppler pause above mid-ocean wave,
parsing my self going the other way,
dulcet is what soothes,
faux longing on Channel Five,
piped accent sliding towards the universal,
Afro-Americo-Euro-
oh, oh, so horizontal elevator cuisine,
East is...and West is...
and never...and always...

Amidst the polar stars, groping our way
along the edge
of this fragile celestial carapace,
we locate ourselves

by satellite and triangulation,
plastic utensil and free drinks,
by hemisphere and the nonspecific,
the direction water flows,
by the setting back of time, hour by hour,
the slight declension in the colour of skin

the loss of a vowel,
swallowing of a consonant,
by the inchward progress,
self-erasing tilt and swivel,
the tug and pull,
heart-flip missed beat
of the digital plane
on a blank screen.

# JUST PASSING THROUGH

## Da Capo

I ride the varicosed splay of arterials
past bricked facades,
tipsters, hawkers, bettors, barristers, brokers,
greased chipsters, cobbled markets,
torn cul-de-sacs

past cracked Rastas, urban disasters,
past masters, and their slaves

unhurried *Krishnas,* their kin,
parishioners, missionaries, unlovable, unsaved

East-Enders, pretenders, blind-deaf defenders
of the faith,
unkempt, undreamt, all
who've lost face.

I kneel in the shadow of Doric certitude.

Pigeon shit weeps from Nelson's unseeing eye,
caroms off the city's crumbling columns.
History's false profits, solemn slumlords,
claim to take the hit
for sterling's sudden fall.

Emptied mansions hammer home
smashed toilet bowls in dandelion yards,
refuge to the hapless, the just-happened-along.

Eden to the exiled multiplicity,
splendid squalor, burned retinal reminder
of what has been,
what is to come, *polis in extremis.*

A carousel of listless clichés — smoke, chaos, revenge —
circles the city.

The capital is ablaze,
Burger King re-igniting the revolution,
plunging the heart of Empire
into darkness.

And I

I cash in the flipped coin of childhood
for small talk and diaspora fare
— *rollmops, sauerkraut* —
aftertaste of nostalgia flooding my tongue's salted tributaries.

And see
see, that's me,
me just passing through,
after all

for it is cold as heaven
and cold comfort,
eking out a living here.

## Segue

If the flight west was an answer to the riddle,
a softening of hard truths,
and the journey east a recasting of the question,
this turn south is a shiv beneath the skin,
leaving no mark,
save an exit wound...

## Caesura

I stole past the Sphinx
not on four legs, nor two,
nor even three

sank into the dark continent
down through an oval frame of desert,
unravelling in the twisted wind

crashed through the unwound dusk, melted twilight,
where the sea poured itself
into the splayed throat of the Nile

carrying within me three identities,
all false,
so the land would not recognize my face,
unmask me

vorticed amongst the loosed souls
in the dust-swept courtyards
of the City of the Dead

stirred the nipple-tipped rushes
that fringed the continent's dark oesophagus.

I heard,
through the tattered flapping of the dhows' white sails,
the whispered names of motherless princes, long dead,
who

unmoored from home,
stumbled through the dark-eyed desert,
who

thinking they could follow the eternal thread of longing
to its sunken source,
drank, instead,
from the dried breast of their own nostalgia

who, having solved the riddle's surface question,
drowned in its depth,
sank below the wind-clasped mollusk of sand
that shifted beneath their feet.

*After forty years*
*—in the caesura before the final descent—*
*did you lose heart,*
*knowing that what you had become*
*meant that you could come no further?*

*Knowing that the long exile from home*
*was, in fact, the journey home,*
*did you pause*
*before plunging your mother's clasp*
*into your own deceiving pupils?*

*Did you—watching the white cloth*
*unwind from her naked body, its slow fall*
*into gravity's grasp—*
*at last see*
*that blindness was the way to sight?*

Adrift in the city's mad marketplace
—amid lantern hiss, hookah swirl, pomegranate sweetness—
did *I* not see,
as I stooped to gather the flatbread and fresh tomato
from the still warm press
of a dark woman's hands

having refused the welcome home
offered by a boy for a small price

did I not see
that this was the road back to the promised land?

If so, what was the promise made?

## Segue (cont'd)

…my eyes, restless with remorse,
track the archeology of regress.

After a night of restlessness,
the tender sun,
bright and cold above Kilimanjaro's white nipple,
approaches dawn,
lights my way home.

The world separates again —
light and dark.

# SUNT LACRIMAE RERUM

## Prayer

They called it the age of exploration.
All you felt was the narrowness of the world.

Day and night,
the taste of salt was on your tongue.
Names sat in your bitter mouth.
For weeks you rode the aphasic current.

As long as you remained at sea
you were safe,
its vastness a finitude, buoyancy a womb.

You had no reason to believe in the world's edge,
nor not to,
yet you steered close to land,
not wanting to test the limits of faith.
The constant horizon an amnesia.

The sea you called *Storms*, the land, *Hope*.
Near landfall, sunken masts swayed like prayers.

You lingered in the cape's open palm,
unsure of your footing.
The sea had left you groundless.

Movement had become stillness,
wave-cradled.

The sea spoke to you through soft lips
lapping at your sides.

When you touched land,
your shadow kneeled to kiss the red earth.

Sharp rocks embedded themselves in your knees,
bruising skin.

You ran your tongue across the rough ground,
its taste of black sweat,
scorpion song, cicadas' scuttle and scurry,
mamba's shuck and jive, ungulates' slow cudding,
*fynbos'* faint shushing.

Wetness from your eyes watered the dry earth,
its scars and sutures.
This was your promised land,
your side-by-side parchment.

Nouns spilled from your tongue,
laying claim to what had been spoken.
Soil found its voice, sang itself into existence.
You pissed into the wind,
felt the warmth of your body, sowed seeds.

Bougainvillea burst pink against the welded sky,
mimosa flecking yellow across bare shoulders,
purple jacaranda *pop-popping* beneath calloused soles.
Scattered *haa-dee-dahs* scored the raucous morning air,
scorched mangoes oozing gold,
silvered litchis leaking sticky across your palms.

Mist spilled down from the mountain — *sunt lacrimae rerum.*

This, the place of the great divide
and great coming together.
You could not tell your skin from the air,
could see in all directions.

Time enters you.
You are capable of anything and nothing.

You follow the curve of the continent's fractured spine
inland, to the north,
where fresh blood sweetens air,
turning rivers red,
spreading across the land with covenantal certainty.

Runnels of smoke rise from smouldering grass,
stubble cutting your blackened feet.
Crickets skitter into dark corners,
carrying their burnt song on their heads.

*Kopjies,* like memory, erode.
*Dongas* bloom and wash away.

Meanwhile, the hyena stalks the chain-link fence,
searching for a breach...

*Bulalani abathagathi!*

## Lament

Last night you pretended to be someone else.
That was only part of it.
The dark had already mistaken you.
You could still pass, though daylight was dangerous.

When you entered enemy territory,
the colour drained from your face,
seeped into the city's streets.
This was a line not to be crossed,
but you slipped under.

You had travelled west, across the escarpment,
past eyeless mud huts, round-shouldered with age,
cattle strung across the *veld,*
parched throats of *mielies* calling out to you,
husked vowels curled back on themselves,
barefoot women bearing wood and water
on their heads.

Pastel *cosmos,* lining the dirt roads,
bowed to you as you passed,
petals feathering your bare legs.
Barbed wire fences thrummed,
telegraphing your coming.

From the hill's brow, you looked back
down the valley.

This is how the land carves out a memory of itself,
a glacial retreat, ground giving in
under the pressure of so much frozen time,
the present evaporating.

When you crossed the border,
no one asked for proof of your name,
or where you'd come from,
though your almond eyes and beaked nose
betrayed your mongrel history.

Had they cracked the spine of your past,
they would have found the ink
still wet on the pages of your skin,
would have heard the deracinated rattle of syllables —
*Ezulwini, District Six, Mhlambanyati* —
scattering in your wake,
drying before they touched ground.

You had travelled north from the Cape,
against nature,
leaving behind the flattened welt of the grey sea,
the lime-whitened walls,
your language still slave to its master.

You had refused the offer of food,
though as soon as you set foot on the road
you could taste the salt of regret on your tongue,
the sweet-sour flotsam of *kedgeree* and *bobotie,*
of *perske blatjang* floating in your mouth,
bitter lament locked in your jaw.

You had thought forgetting would conform
to the logic of distance, but found the inverse
to be true,
absence's algorithm proving that out of sight
only brought to mind,
reversed what the body asserted.

Trying to outdistance your shadow,
you came to the edge of the known world,
to that place where you would either fall into the abyss
or turn on yourself.
You cruised the white beaches
for fresh prey and a new face.

The locals took you in.
You fell in love with the sound of ice.

Like Patroclus, you awoke from winter,
clothed in armour stolen in the night,
and struck out for battle,
only to learn of the inevitable softness of flesh.

When they sliced off your head,
they were only doing your bidding.
When they pried off your helmet,
they were not prepared for what they saw.
When they kissed you on the lips,
they could not help themselves.
When they attached the electrodes to your heart,
they could not find a beat.
When they removed the needle from your arm,
you fell into a dream.
When they abandoned you on the island,
they wrapped you in white sails.
When they set fire to the faggots,
it was only a pyrrhic victory.

You turned to ash in their mouths.

The light rose,
the sky brushed with birdsong.

# THE EARTH OPENING

# Echo

I return

to the crumbling houses of widows,
where keys bunch like thieves at wary doorways,
faded birds on cupboard doors stand guard
over smudged glasses and crystallized liqueurs

to where carpets are worn to the warp
and remnants of burnt toast
burnish the air with their scrapings,
locks all face inwards,
and a small boy lies face down
on his bed, dreaming of his best friend's mother's breasts
bobbing like plucked apples
on clouded bathwater

to where a murderer-rapist sees his ebony face
on the front page of the *Johannesburg Star,*
*Final Edition,*
eye half swollen-closed
above the terrible statistics of his life,
where German-Jewish widows declare their hands
beneath the pointed shade of a eucalyptus tree

where, in skin's soft embrace,
the tip of a broken pencil lies embedded
like memory

## Paean

Falling
from the pink tongues,
from the caliginous mouths of pale madams,
death, decay, Cimmerian anarchy
unbound, unleashed hunger overspilling
the dammed walls, flooding the dry plains,
the trickle of poverty
pouring out in another tongue.

There has been rain, each afternoon at three,
and there will be more,
every day,
with sub-tropical regularity.

The reservoirs are full, and here —
in the nipple of the great mother's breast —
all of Africa is pooling.

Designer banana trees dip and sway their fringed skirts,
hems brushing the tops of electrified walls.

Through the battened morning
I careen past buildings emptied of people
and memory.

The cars asleep, four abreast,
safely off the streets,
concertina barricades severing the civic from the civil,
visible signs of retreat and advance.
Cocky gun and cocked-grin glance.

On the corner, a man known as *Boy*
peddles pink penny bubble-gum wrapped in life's riddles,

knifes a *pawpaw* in two,
stunning amber flesh, spilling black seed.

A tank, cemented in time,
aims its sterile turret longingly
at the recent past.
The banks have double doors for single entry.

The girls and boys,
wearing different hues of awkwardness,
serve coloured juices in the mango shade.

*AAAAAyyyy mieLIES!*
The hunched song of the old woman,
spilling from her basket,
fills my captive ear.

Music emporium jazz decants into the street,
bent and curved and barely hanging
together,
Zakes' sweet sax a eulogy to all that is blood
and loss,
Dludlu's torn guitar chords
blurring, swaying, erasing.

I wander in a tight circle of safety
through white malls, past black carvings,
visitor in a land of careless homogenization
and carefree slaughter,
spending what I don't have.

And still,
the domestic morning mumbles, close-mouthed,
stirs in its whitewashed quarters,
thick *pap* and sweet tea,
the earth opening,
red and sweet and wet.

# O, HOW THEY LOVED ME

## Blessing

O, how they loved me,
each in their own way,
until the storm swept over the *veld,*
choreographing dust across the paint-by-numbers sky,
drowning the swallows
dark beneath the clouds.

How I followed their cues and loops,
straying between careful lines,
as if a sinew held me to this tight calligraphy,
this telephone-wire tension.

At times I was beyond their reach,
out of bounds.

Who's to blame for that extra step?
For the spindrels of dust
rising from the yellowing mine-dumps
spooned out across the Witwatersrand,
bruising the late sky?
For the image
of some mother's aproned arse
bent over the white stove?

For the taste of sliced onions
on white butter bread,
dusted with black pepper?

Who's sifting through the particulate?

## Ligature

Severed by the nightly news,
the currency of a free fall,
I remember, this is a country of farewells,
unanswered calls.

I had given up suffering, I thought,
left behind on the runway
together with my unmarked ballot,
a voice I knew still calling.

But flesh remembers, where skin forgets.
My left thumb bore the brunt
of my right hand's despair.

How this sacrifice saved me from numbness,
but left a scar across your body.

How you tended to my torn hand,
your careful stitches
a way of bringing us together.

How my hand went in search
of the curved cleft of your left nipple,
rising from the sunken, pale plateau of your breast,
up the wide white breadth of your abdomen.

How you capitulated
to the only thing we had in common: skin.

How you yielded like an unwatered flower,
which still did you no good.

How I return to the scene of the crime,
as though it held some truth.

## Lullaby

Her memory slips.

I ran my fingers across her scars,
her adumbrated skin,
her hieroglyphs of pain.

She took me by the hand,
led me through the two-dimensional hangings
in her gallery,
but still,
I could not move my feet.

She offered me her records,
but still,
I could not scratch out a song.

We danced drunkenly on the hotel's parapet,
to the hum of the neon sign,
courting gravity.

*I don't do the dark,* she said, *at least don't do it well.*
*Light hurts my eyes,* I replied, *night's where I choose to dwell.*

## Quaver (Penelope)

I could hear the women keening,
their dying ululations.

I would tend to her,
my ear tuned to her,
a catch in my throat.

How I remember it,
as a draining out,
a clutch in the jug's thin neck.

I would pour myself out of her.

Make no mistake.
Just because her curves lent me form,
she was no willow.

She was the spinner, the whetting stone.
She sent me off to war.
Madness was my refuge, sanity my unmade bed.
I could no more plough through it

I lay in the furrows,
sliced open my hand, bled into the evening.
The soil turned dark.

When the ploughshare cleaved the earth,
something broke.
Staked through their hearts,
plants leant into each other
for comfort.

This offhand god, off-duty, off-kilter,
raged, raged against night's fall.

She declined,
her legs crossed,
her thread unstitched.

# Elegy

Her bed bears the impress
of an unhurried leave-taking, the promise,
or lie, of return.

Women come and go, pausing
to insert keys
and condolences.

Beware of beds.
Beware of empty beds.
Beware of beds rooted to the spot

that demand proof of identity
after prolonged abstinence and absence,
that charge the blood-price
of unrequited lovers' lives.

Beware of beds that hold hands
fumbling for sanctuary
amidst the wet folds of adolescence.

Beware the unfinished book
at the head of the bed,
open at the place you first learned to be unforgiving,
the page you became hostage to fate.

## Lullaby II

Light falls like regret across the sheets' furrows,
shadows banked against my coming.
She stirs, disturbing the white.

She is an island, afloat,
her dress a dark sail.

When — at last — I find her,
I find her wanting.

She blames herself.

I would sooner throttle my throat
than sing her desert song.

Apology catches on my dumb heart,
losing its voice to cut chords and slack veins.
Somewhere calls.
Hope feints.

She is the unmarked grave at which I must mourn,
bend my head.

She whispers, *getfucked.*

# THE PLACES SHE DIDN'T TOUCH ME

## Bridge

Whether to follow the image of the one-eyed man,
glasses pasted to his shattered face,
or the hurried crowd that moved in both directions.

From here it was downhill,
either way.

Shifting my weight,
I took up residence on borrowed floors,
tested marriages before they had begun,
overstayed my welcome.

No evidence of this time remains,
no black-and-whites, no negatives,
trace elements.
Save for the ways in which no one writes to each other.

As if they ever did.

I would like to remember the canals,
or what I would imagine them to have been,
their gentle arc and gypsy curves,
the plod of heavy hooves past Sunday pubs

not the view below the waterline,
workmen stripped to their pink waists
peeling back the river's blackened skin,
exhuming the porous skeleton
of a conqueror's silted quay.
You *can* step in the same river twice.

Tell *that* to the cuckold who held a lit match to my face.
Was that before
or after I had made love to his bride-to-be?

She preferred not to kiss me
on the mouth, but afterwards, bathed with me
in the warm waters of her lover's stilled house.

Still, there were things she would not betray,
promises yet to be made.

I would like to remember the sweet curve
of her ear, the Englishness of her skin.
Her name.
The porcelain splash of water
battering the white tub against the blue roar of the gas jets.

The places she didn't touch me...

## Siren Song

On the *via dolorosa*,
the stations of the cross — King's, Charing —
reflected in the epileptic light,
I caught a broken glimpse of her Gorgon mask,
saw how her life was a sigh,
a reprimand,
a demand.
The world too small for her.

Saw how men wanted her body,
her skill with things,
the rest, excess.

She was the other half,
the ouroboros' mouth swallowing my tale,
my song of exile.

When I lapsed into the forbidden language of childhood,
she cut out my tongue,
added me to her quiver of causes,
offered — in exchange — a floor, a mattress,
a lady-in-waiting.

There is no end to this,
this perfect circle,
infinite geometry of betrayal.

*There is a way,* she said, *to get back.*
*You must start with the body and,*
*with the body, end.*

*But you cannot go home*
*yet*

*again.*

And because the salt sea,
before spewing me up
onto this wretched, fog-bound spit of land,
had blinded me to all but the surface of things,
I took this to be true.

*Men are the enemy,* she mouthed,
as she fucked her casual lover.
She taught me that property is theft,
tore my name from me
as we rose up, refugees in search of a home.

When, at last, I found myself,
I was on the floor of the cutting room.
Clotho, Lachesis, Atropos,
spun out, my measure taken, cut off,
compelled, once more, to live
with the end in mind.

# THE GATES HAVE WINGS

## Descant

What you get is what you see.
Greys of shade.

Your arm around my shoulder,
my back to the wall,
showered by a sibilant light.

From the kitchen,
tintinnabulation of rice and rock across sundisk.
Raised voices.

No shadow crosses the sibling floor,
the stalk of faceless silence.

I am story and pen,
remembered and remembering,
spooned against your bare back
in the lightning night,
beneath the silhouette sweep of leaves.

I am the chosen,
not of my choosing.

When I draw breath,
blue water fills my lungs.

Colour muddies the waters,
sky and earth bleeding charcoal into sienna.

It's plain to see that I am already dead,
that lines emerge from my open mouth
like the bars of a graph.

And, being dead, it is easy to blame.

Life is lived here, in the eclipse,
the shadowplay of sparrows spinning light,
wingdarts across the page.

These things run deeper than blood
even,
something cellular,
the slowing
of the heart.

When I had you as tether,
I could fly,
but losing the thread, I just kite away.

Over my shoulder,
God's finger points the way;
this way, I know the reason.

The lawn comes to an abrupt edge.
The gates have wings.
I see this in my dreams,
this ambivalent angel, cemented to the earth.

What sadness in those downturned feathers.
What night.

# Psalm

It is only half true what they say
about the boy and the country.

After the equivalent number of years
plus one,
the temporal balance is tipped,
the particular drains, fails to locate itself,
gets caught in shadows.

The sharp edge of familial sounds
that poison the back of the throat, break apart.
The guttural, glottal *g*,
the *ach* and *du* of the goose step that stalked you
across the Atlantic.

Like Abel, after he was murdered,
you were given refuge, a gun,
a certificate that said, *friendly enemy alien.*

With a yellow *Magen David*
no longer stitched to your sleeve,
you rose
up the glass tower that concentrated the sun,
so that moles spread black
on the tender yellow skin
of the Indian grocer's mangoes across the street,
and they became good only for feeding pigs
and the starving.

After you took your lone seat
in the dark-panelled chamber,
where democracy was slaughtered afresh daily

as you mouthed
*Our Father, who art in heaven…*
from monday to friday,
and *Baruch atah Adonai…*
on saturday

even then,
you would never quite find,
nor forget,
your place.

## Kaddish

Though the day is only half dressed,
buildings still dark,
the city lies through its teeth.

I hear the streetcars whispering,
going over their lines.

Morning's suit sags at the shoulders.

I search the city's pockets for a key,
try to find myself on the freshly creased streets,
get lost in their folds.

But,
when I stand quite still,
I can hear the stones of the old synagogue give way
beneath history's boot,
bombs fold into the panicked geometry of the city,
the snuffing out of stars.

Outside the *bar mleczny* I join the bastard line
still drunk on last night's vodka.
We are waiting for history's judgement,
for a bowl of subsidized *borscht*.

You have come here from the east, bareheaded,
your *kippa* tucked into your worn belt.
In the empty graveyard, you kneel down
before the graffitied tombstones, black *Swastikas* still wet
to the touch.

In the temple,
I join the aged sitting *shiva*,
mourning the sacrifice of the young.

I am the prodigal tourist.
I stand across the street.
They have torn down the front steps to widen the road,
but left the concrete bunker standing.

A shutter clatters open as morning clears its throat.
The latticed neck of a crane stretches out
over black water.

The river mouths *remember,*
the streets sign *forget.*

# MY HEART, SURFACING TOO FAST

## Harmony

*And did those feet in ancient time,*
*Walk upon England's mountains green?*

And did those feet find refuge here,
in the crook of the arm of the Severn,
on the sweep of the tide that bore me this far inland,
where the river narrowed, turned back on itself,
beneath the cooling towers,
dark Satanic mills?

For forty days I took to bed, until the flood
had subsided,
until the old sow had cleared the land,
square by electrified square,
uprooting nettles with her leathered snout.

When I rose again,
the mistress of the farmhouse baked bread, teased me, gently:
*Mother, I have tried and cried...*
*Tried it your way*
*Now I'll do it my way...*

In the kitchen, her ex-husband-to-be brewed dark tea,
licked the parched hem of his fag,
complained of the failures of his children.

I eddied there,
caught in the stillness
between revolutions.

Over a half-drained pint of bitter,
a man, a boy really,

who had never ventured beyond the narrow openings
of this dry lagoon,
said through the skim of foam on his upper lip,
*I admire Hitler...*

This patchwork was coming apart,
stitching of moss-stoned walls, broken.

When I returned to the farmhouse,
on the wall above the sink,
above the endlessness of dirtied dishes,
I painted the punch-line of a standing joke:
*In perpetuam...*

Using milk bottles and a straightened wire clothes hanger,
I learned to divine for water,
unearthed a taste, but not a talent,
for the occult, searched in the mirror,
in the image above the candle flame,
for the face of another, some evidence of a centre.

Sisyphus put his raw shoulder to the wheel,
clavicle hollowing to the arc of the rock,
shoulder and boulder coming to know each other.

One day, his feet paused
at the generous iron gate that swung open on its own,
between dirt road and farm.

One day, what had been, until then
the only question,
was answered,
at last, by an act of kindness.

What remained was the trace of the gate's sweep,
crumpled imprint on sheets,
roughness of bread,
coarse harmonies sung off-key...

*Take a load off Fanny, take a load for me,*
*Take a load off Fanny, and (...and)*
*you put the load (... put the load)*
*right on me...*

# Anthem (O Canada)

The first time I set eyes on you,
you were laid out flat,
east to west.

You had no depth, no past.
You had not suffered,
or could not hear it yet.

So I taught you to listen for loss,
in the wooden echo of an axe,
in the blanketed folds of snow,
in the ice that cracked beneath your weight,
swallowing you whole,
in the nuggets of dreams that failed to pan out.

I had first learned to read you through touch,
through the dark vein of a blunt pencil
pressing down into your transparent traces,
outlining your crenellated coastal complications,
your squared prairie certainties.

When first I set foot on you, you were naked,
doubled through water's refraction.
I dipped a tentative toe into your labial folds,
got caught in the matted shoals,
the rough creases.

Even so, at first your hold on me was tenuous,
fragile.
The tide tugged at me.

On certain days,
when the clouds pulled back from the mountains,

the angle of light played tricks on my eyes.
The birds, singing in a foreign tongue,
would fool my homesick ear.
Only the relentless green persisted.

I grew sick on so much fecundity,
so much unbroken promise.
My neck grew stiff, searching for the sky.
My eyes, grown used to walls,
lost focus.
My heart, surfacing too fast,
collapsed into weightlessness.

Over time,
I drifted farther and farther inland,
to where trees touched sky,
their roots stretched out in shallow graves,
any sudden wind laying them flat,
baring their snake-strung souls.

I lay down, resting my head
on a pillow of rot.
Leaves filled my ears with their fallen song.
Needles punctured the permafrost, marking a tattoo of the earth,
a disappearing map of the future,
on the soft underside of my skin.

I boarded the train east,
crossed unremarked boundaries,
slipped through tunnels and passes,
towards something approaching forgiveness.

Slept,
sitting upright for five days and nights,
watching the country grow smaller,
close in around me.

I saw what they meant.

I shared bread and cheese with the family across the aisle,
the children opening me up with their naked eyes.
The heat poured in from the Great Lakes,
spread through my pores,
washing the Pacific salt from my wounds.

The news from the west, from beyond the Rockies,
was that you had been at the wheel,
and that the wheel had been unforgiving.

What had been taken?

The Sudan sky,
the corrugated night we sweated through,
crows, white bibs tucked into their black vests,
toying with a mottled hawk,
the hidden passport,
promise of the Cairo night,
prophecy of the stars,
the *kwashiorkor* children running their fingers
over the freckled braille on your pale arms,
mourning-sickness, your body neatly serrated
into so many prime cuts,
the Okavango song, wondering where the lions are,
a broken premise,
the possibility of an ending.

And what's left in their place?

When first I laid a hand on you,
you had no shape,
save that of my fist.

# Cry

I remember a time
when the continents still touched,
the rivers ran together,
before the land split apart.

I hold the wound of this land close to my heart,
if only to give me purchase,
something to push against.

Welcome me home, though I come in disguise,
though I have been gone long.

Run your fingers across the map of my heart,
its contours and *kopjies,*
its opened veins and bent arteries,
hardened to the shape of its promise.

You are right, of course, to hold back,
to keep the door closed.

I carry the smell of other countries,
strange foods, foreign women.

You are my dark continent,
my red earth,
my unbroken chain,
my severed hand,
my child soldier,
my shantytown,
my blood diamond.

You are my cry in the night,
the farewell in the river's fall,
its Rapunzel twist over the precipice.

You are the broken finger of rock
splintering the morning sun,
the loosened cuticle of granite,
the swallowed scream — wife, child, kettle —
disappearing through cloud's false floor.

You are the god-driven wagon
pulled towards something called home,
the hoofed beasts shaking their great horned heads
at the impossible descent,
mudded waves lapping at the sky,
vertiginous echo lost in the mountain fog.

Remember,
in the making of this,
that lives were lost,
limbs torn, bodies twisting slowly
as the blades of a tired fan on a hot afternoon

a winnowing oar, separating this moment
from its husk.

## Cadence

Having been schooled in the architecture of loss,
I drew blueprints of the blues,
erected whole cities of sadness,
took up room in suites of sorrow.

I walked in on you.
*You act as if your life is already over,*
you were saying.

The suitors asleep or slain,
the bed, rooted,
empty.

No wind to lean into,
no past to fall back on,
no present to speak of,

how can I know what I feel
until I touch its rough edge;
what I think,
until I give it voice,
burn myself on the ash of a sentence
left hanging?

Having evolved from groan to noun,
howl to hope,
the tyranny of the imagined,
the futility of the future tense

this refugee song splits
in two,
its long shadow casting me out.

# Key

***"Oh what greater happiness…"***—From a "poem constructed from fragments of lost works by Sophocles, from the March issue of *Poetry* [2007]. The fragments, from papyrus manuscripts or quoted in the writings of later authors, were selected, assembled, and translated by Reginald Gibbons, who teaches at Northwestern University." *Harper's Magazine*, June 2007 (pp. 18-19).

## Call

***lowveld*** *(Afrikaans)*—Sub-tropical grass and wetland in the former South African province of (Eastern) Transvaal, now *Mpumalanga*, "the place where the sun rises."

***mielies*** *(Afrikaans)*—Maize, corn.

***proteas***—National flower of South Africa.

## Da Capo

***polis*** *[Greek]*—Greek city state. (*cf.* Charles Olson: *"so few/ have the polis/ in their eye"* from the *Maximus Poems,* Edited by George F. Butterick. 1985. University of California Press.).

## Caesura

**City of the Dead**—"City" within a city built to house the dead in Cairo.

## Prayer

***Sunt lacrimae rerum*** *(Latin)*—*"sunt lacrimae rerum et mentem mortalia tangunt."* "These are the tears of things, and our mortality cuts to the heart" (Virgil: the *Aeneid*). Also translated as "there are tears for things," or even "the tears that are in things." Spoken by Aeneas through his tears on seeing a mural in a Carthaginian temple depicting the Trojan War and deaths of his friends and countrymen.

**mambas**—The green and black mamba, related to the cobra and native to Africa, are amongst the world's deadliest snakes.

*fynbos* *(Afrikaans—Lit. "fine-bush.")* Natural vegetation unique to a thin band of land along South Africa's South-West coast. Characterized by hardy, low growing plants, including the *protea,* a good sampling of *fynbos* can be seen covering the wind-blown top of Cape Town's iconic Table Mountain.

*Kopjies* *(Afrikaans; plural—Lit. "little-heads").* Also spelled (and pronounced, in the singular) *koppie* or *kopje (Dutch).* Low, flat-topped hill or rocky outcrop, similar to the North American *mesa.*

*Dongas* *(Anglo-Indian; plural)*—Dry gullies caused by soil erosion, a common feature of the drought-stricken South African landscape. The loose, brittle soil is vulnerable to flood, drought, high winds, and poor cultivation practices.

*haa-dee-dahs* *(Onomatopoeia)*—Large grey-brown-olive ibis, named for its raucous cry.

**the great mountain**—Table Mountain

*Bulalani abatagathi!* *(Zulu)*— *"Kill the wizards!"* In their trek into the interior of Southern Africa, away from the hated British who governed the Cape, the Dutch *voortrekkers* (pioneers) encountered and fought with African tribes on whose lands they were planning to settle, meeting their fiercest opposition from the Zulus. One of the *voortrekker* leaders, Piet Retief, arranged a meeting with the great Zulu king, Dingaan, to negotiate the granting of land to the *trekkers.* After the negotiations, as the Zulus were preparing to bid farewell, Retief and his men were asked to leave their weapons outside of the compound as a gesture of respect. While the Zulu warriors danced, Dingaan shouted *"Bulalani abatagathi!"* Retief and his men were seized, bound and put to death, Retief being the last to die. One (literal) explanation given for the killing is that, the night before, Zulu warriors heard the sound of hooves outside the *great kraal,* and because Zulu wizards were believed to ride on hyenas, the Zulus thought that the white man's wizards rode on horses. If there were any sound of hooves, it was likely simply that of the *voortrekkers'* stray horses. Just as likely, Dingaan, no fool, guessed at what the coming of the white man would mean to his land and his people and seized the opportunity to try to eliminate this threat. If so, the subsequent history of South Africa demonstrated both his prescience and, in the short-term, his failure. In the long run, however, Dingaan's people can claim a victory of sorts with the overturning of *apartheid* and the election of Jacob Zuma, a Zulu, to the South African presidency.

## Lament

***cosmos***— Fragile-looking but hardy, this wild flower blooms resplendent and plentiful in northern South Africa alongside country roads in the narrow strip between farm fence and highway. When cut, they do not survive long.

***Ezulwini*** *(siSwati).* Pronounced *Eh-zool-weenie.* — *Heaven.* The Ezulwini Valley (Valley of Heaven) is a vast, fertile, flat-bottomed, glacial gorge in Swaziland, a landlocked country bordered on three sides by South Africa and on the fourth by Mocambique. An independent nation since 1968, Swaziland was a former British Protectorate, having sought protection under the British Crown from warring Afrikaner *voortrekkers* moving north and inland to settle. During the apartheid years, many temporary migrant workers came from Swaziland and other neighbouring countries to South Africa. While most of these would have been indigenous Africans, some would have been people of mixed-race, so-called "coloureds," classified as such by the apartheid regime. Some of the lighter skinned "coloureds" would have been able to "pass" as white in South Africa.

***District Six***— Former vibrant inner-city residential area in Cape Town, inhabited primarily by so-called "coloureds." Best known for the forced removal of over 60,000 of its inhabitants during the 1970's by the South African government. In 2003, work was begun to rebuild District Six.

***Mhlambanyati*** *(siSwati)* Pronounced *Mm-shlum-bun-yahti.* — Town in Swaziland.

***kedgeree*** *(Indian)* **and** ***bobotie*** *(Indonesian)* — Respectively curried fish and rice, and curried minced-meat (ground beef) and egg, these dishes were introduced to South Africa by *Malay* slaves (mostly Javanese from Indonesia) brought over on ships by the Dutch East India Company. *Cape Malays* are a distinctive subgroup of the so-called "coloured" community living in and around Cape Town.

***perske blatjang*** *(Afrikaans: peach + Javanese: "blachang," chutney)* — Sweet and spicy. The best *blatjang* to have with your curry or *samosa* is Mrs. Ball's Original Recipe Chutney.


## Paean

***pawpaw***— papaya.

**Zakes…Dludlu** — Black South African jazz musicians, Bra (Brother) Zakes, pianist and Jimmy Dludlu, guitarist.

*pap (Afrikaans:* aka *mielie pap, mielie meal, samp)* — Cooked corn meal, a staple of the black South African diet. Not generally eaten by whites.

## Blessing

**mine-dumps** — Large man-made hills of fine yellow sand, crushed tailings from the gold mining process.

*Witwatersrand (Afrikaans — Lit. "The ridge of white waters").* A line of hills in Northern South Africa, running East-West, at the centre of which lies the city of Johannesburg. These hills sit atop the world's richest gold-bearing reef.

## Siren Song

**Ouroboros** *[Greek]* — Mythological serpent or dragon forming a circle swallowing its own tail.

**Clotho, Lachesis, Atropos** *[Greek]* — The three Fates (*moirae*) from Greek mythology; respectively, she who spins the thread of each life, she who measures that thread, and she who cuts it.

## Psalm

*Magen David (Hebrew)* — *Star of David.* In Hitler's Germany, Jews were forced to wear a yellow cloth *Magen David* to allow for easy identification.

*friendly enemy alien (Oxymoron)* — Official designation given to German-Jewish refugees in South Africa during the war.

**the glass tower** — The Johannesburg Stock Exchange.

**the dark-panelled chamber** — South African Parliament, Cape Town.

*Baruch atah Adonai…* *(Hebrew)* — *"Blessed are You, Lord our God…"*

## Kaddish

**bar mleczny** *(Polish—Lit. "milk bar")* Low-cost, state-subsidized restaurants, serving meals consisting primarily of vegetables, carbohydrates and dairy, with no or little costly meat and frequented mostly by students and the elderly poor. Products of the Communist era, these eateries remained popular in post-Communist Poland.

**kippa** *(Yiddish:* aka *yarmulke)*—Jewish skullcap.

**shiva** *(Hebrew—Lit. "seven")* The week-long period of grief and mourning for family members of the deceased.

## Harmony

**And did those feet...**—William Blake, from the preface to his epic poem, *Milton. (The Illuminated Books of William Blake, Volume 5: Milton, A Poem.* Editors, Robert N. Essick, Joseph Viscomi. 1998. Princeton University Press.) Also, first lines of the hymn, *Jerusalem* (1916), music by Sir Hubert Parry.

**Mother I have tried and cried...**—Joan Armatrading, *Give It A Try* (from her first album, *Whatever's For Us,* 1972).

**Take a load off Fanny...**—The Band, from *The Weight.* (Written by Robbie Robertson. From *The Band's* debut album, *Music From Big Pink.* 1968. Capitol Records).

## Anthem ( O Canada )

**kwashiorkor** *(Kwa/Ghanaian)*—Childhood disease of malnutrition, characterized by a large, distended potbelly. Completely preventable, it is endemic amongst children in poverty and drought-stricken parts of Africa. Its literal meaning is "the one who is displaced."

**wondering where the lions are**—Bruce Cockburn, *Wondering Where The Lions Are* (from *Dancing in the Dragon's Jaws,* 1979. True North Records).

# Acknowledgements

"Lament" is dedicated to the memory of Alan Lomberg.

"Harmony" is for Jenny Yates.

"Anthem (O Canada)" is dedicated to the memory of Penne Davidson.

Much gratitude to Betsy Warland, for reading a series of early drafts of these poems, for her experienced poet's eye and musical ear, and for her skill and insight as both reader and teacher, which greatly helped me to shape a loose collection of unpolished poems into a coherent whole. Profound appreciation to George Payerle, for his excitement about and support for these poems, for his fine poet's sensibility and firm editorial hand, and for convincing me to sometimes (but not always) let go of my "wilful obscurity." Thanks also for introducing me to the best Greek roast lamb in Vancouver. Many thanks to Karen Haughian at Signature Editions for publishing this, my first book, and for steering me through the process of publication. Much thanks to Kate Braid, for her encouragement and for sharing her wealth of knowledge and experience about the world of Canadian poetry.

I am deeply grateful to all those, too many to name but none forgotten, who accompanied, supported and challenged me along the various journeys recounted in these poems.

And all my love and heartfelt gratitude to my wife, Debbie, whose love, patience, caring and simple presence made and make all of this possible. Debbie, you are my home and new found land.

## About the Author

Lawrence Feuchtwanger has had a varied and interesting career. He has been a journalist, tree-planter, baker and counsellor. Born in Johannesburg, South Africa, he immigrated to Canada in 1976 after two years of living in England and travelling overland through Africa, from Egypt to Southern Africa. He lives in Vancouver with his Canadian-born wife, near his children and grandchildren.

Eco-Audit
*Printing this book using Rolland Opaque 50
instead of virgin fibres paper saved the following resources:*

| Trees | Solid Waste | Water | Air Emissions |
|-------|-------------|-------|---------------|
| 1 | 19 kg | 1,564 L | 176 kg |